MONSTERS

ROBOTS

BY DON NARDO

KIDHAVEN PRESS

An imprint of Thomson Gale, a part of The Thomson Corporation

THOMSON
————✦————™
GALE

Detroit • New York • San Francisco • New Haven, Conn. • Waterville, Maine • London

THOMSON

————————✦———————— ™

GALE

© 2008 Thomson Gale, a part of The Thomson Corporation.

Thomson and Star Logo are trademarks and Gale and KidHaven Press are registered trademarks used herein under license.

For more information, contact
KidHaven Press
27500 Drake Rd.
Farmington Hills, MI 48331-3535
Or you can visit our Internet site at http://www.gale.com

LIBRARY OF CONGRESS CATALOGING-IN-PUBLICATION DATA

Nardo, Don.
    Robots / by Don Nardo.
      p. cm. -- (Monsters)
    Includes bibliographical references and index.
    ISBN 978-0-7377-3779-0 (hardcover)
    1. Robots--Juvenile literature. 2. Androids--Juvenile literature. 3. Stage props--Juvenile literature. 4. Cinematography--Special effects--Juvenile literature. I. Title.
    TJ211.2.N37 2007
    629.8'92--dc22

                                                                2007024361

ISBN-10: 0-7377-3779-4
Printed in the United States of America

CONTENTS

CHAPTER 1

ROBOTS IN FILMS

A **robot** is a mechanical creature or being. Robots are among the scariest and most dangerous monsters that have appeared in movies and television programs. Filmmakers have shown robots destroying houses and other buildings. Other movie robots have chased, injured, or even killed innocent people. And some of these creatures have threatened to destroy the entire human race.

RUTHLESS ROBOTS

A Cylon is one example of a dangerous robot. In the popular current television series *Battlestar Galactica*, humans made the Cylon robots to act as workers and servants. But the Cylons turned against their makers. Most of the humans were killed and the last few left alive had to constantly battle against the Cylons to survive.

Friendly Robots

Not all movie robots are bad, however. Some are useful and courageous. Others are funny and help to lighten a dangerous or grim situation. Two famous examples of good movie robots are R2-D2 and C-3PO, who were featured in the six *Star Wars* films. In the popular 1960s television series *Lost in Space*, a robot also became famous for shouting "Warning! Warning!" to alert its human masters to harm.

It is not always easy to recognize good and bad movie robots. The Cylons, for example, started out good and then became bad. Sometimes both good and bad robots appear together in the same movie or television show. For example, R2-D2 and C-3PO help to fight an army of evil robots in the fifth *Star Wars* film, *Attack of the Clones* (2002). You often need to think about good movie robots when you are looking for the bad ones!

Human Features

There are many different types of movie robots. Some are made to look like humans. Others have just a few human features. For example, the warrior Cylons and C-3PO have a head, a torso, two arms, and two legs. However, unlike humans, these body

R2-D2 (shown left) and C-3PO (standing right) are good movie robots that appeared in all six of the Star Wars films.

Robots

parts are stiff and made of metal or plastic. C-3PO's "skin," for example, is made of gold-colored metal plates. His "eyes" are lights and his metal "lips" do not move when he speaks.

Another famous movie robot, Robby, from *Forbidden Planet* (1956), does not have eyes or lips. His "head" is a see-through globe filled with moving parts. And the "hands" at the ends of his flexible metal arms are like pincers.

ANDROIDS

In contrast, other movie robots are made to look exactly like people. They have eyebrows, eyelashes, and fingernails. They talk, walk, and act very much like people. These realistic human robots are often called **androids**. (The term *android* comes from the Greek word for "man-like." The French novelist Auguste Villiers first used this word in his 1886 book *Tomorrow's Eve*.) In films, the main difference between androids

Some robots appear to be almost human, like the android called Data, pictured here, from the Star Trek: The Next Generation *television series.*

and people is that androids were built whereas humans were born.

One of the most famous movie and television androids is called Data. He is from the crew of the starship *Enterprise* in *Star Trek: The Next Generation*. Played by actor Brent Spiner, Data is the starship's chief operations officer. During the series we discover that he was created by a brilliant scientist, Dr. Noonien Soong. His "brain" is a complex computer, so Data can reason and communicate in a way similar to humans. In a number of episodes, Data saves his fellow crewpersons or the starship from destruction.

Dangerous Androids

In films there tend to be more bad androids than good ones. One example is Data's own "evil twin," Lore. Lore is the result of one of Soong's failed experiments and is always trying to cause trouble.

An even more dangerous and frightening android is the T-1000 from the 1991 blockbuster *Terminator 2: Judgment Day*. The T-1000 is made of a special liquid metal that allows it to take on any shape. This android can pretend to be someone else, which fools many people. What is even more dangerous is that guns cannot stop the T-1000. The robot simply absorbs the bullets and keeps on going.

Another dangerous human-looking robot appears in the film *Westworld* (1973). Played by the late actor Yul Brynner, this robot is part of

a wild west attraction at an amusement park. Unfortunately for the park's visitors, the android goes out of control. Soon it runs wild and kills several people.

NONHUMAN ROBOTS

Other movie robots do not look like humans at all. The *Star Wars* character R2-D2, for example, is a stubby metal canister that rolls along the ground to move. It also squeaks rather than talks. Yet like its friend C-3PO, R2-D2 can think for itself and can perform useful and even heroic acts.

The Daleks from the Dr. Who *television series are ruthless robots whose main purpose is to harm humans.*

The Daleks (pronounced DAH-lecks) are more threatening robots. They appear in the long-running television series *Dr. Who*. A Dalek is shaped like a cone (rather like an oversized salt shaker), with a rotating dome at the top. A mechanical eye sticks out from the dome. The evil Daleks try to burn people by throwing flames or they try to crush their skulls.

A much larger nonhumanoid robot appears in the movie *Kronos* (1957). In the film, an alien space-ship crashes on Earth and a huge machine moves out from the wreckage. This robot is made of two rectangular metal boxes, one suspended above the other, with a small dome perched on the top. Huge piston-shaped supports are attached to the under-side of the lower box. As the pistons begin to move up and down, the **robotic** Kronos travels forward. It terrorizes the countryside and drains energy from power stations, houses, and cities. (It then beams this energy back to its home planet.)

ROBOTIC MOTIVES

Robots come in all shapes and sizes, but they also have a wide range of goals and motives. Some robots, like C-3PO and Data, were programmed

Opposite: A scene from the film The Day the Earth Stood Still *where the alien Klaatu and the robot Gort arrive on Earth. Gort combined elements of both good and bad robots.*

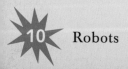

to admire and to help people. In fact, Data often says that he wants to actually *become* human. Other robots, such as the Cylons and Daleks, want to destroy the human race. And Kronos was created to steal the Earth's resources.

Another famous movie robot was designed for a very different reason. In the classic science fiction film *The Day the Earth Stood Still* (1951), a flying saucer lands in Washington, D.C. The human-looking, alien pilot called Klaatu is accompanied by Gort, a robot 10 feet (3m) tall. Made of a silvery metallic material, Gort has a deadly, laser-like ray that easily dissolves tanks, guns, and other weapons. It seems the robot is unstoppable. Klaatu eventually reveals that Gort is one of several robot policemen who patrol outer space. These robots attack and destroy any planet whose people are threatening neighboring planets.

Gort is an example of both a good and a bad movie robot. He was built for good reasons–to maintain the peace. But his power to destroy entire planets makes him a frightening figure. The potential threat of robots to the human race was one of the main features that inspired many early 20th century writers to create robots.

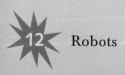

CHAPTER 2

WHERE DID ROBOTS COME FROM?

No one knows for sure where the idea for robots came from. It may have been inspired by ancient myths and folktales about mechanical beings. Perhaps the most famous of these old stories is the Greek myth of Talos. Talos was a mechanical man made of bronze (a mixture of the metals copper and tin). In the myth, Hephestos, god of the forge, creates Talos and gives him to Minos, king of the island of Crete. Talos guards the island from attack. When the hero Jason ventures too close to Crete in his ship, the *Argo*, Talos tosses huge boulders at the boat. But Jason and his crew manage to defeat the bronze giant.

CAPEK'S IDEA

Although Talos can be thought of as an early robot, the actual term *robot* (and the idea of humans making robots themselves) did not appear until the early 20th century. The term comes from a Czech word—*robata,* meaning "forced labor." It was first used by Czech playwright Karel Capek (1890–1938).

In 1920, Capek (pronounced CHOP-eck) wrote a play titled *R.U.R.: Rossum's Universal Robots.* The setting is an island on which a mad inventor named Old Rossum and his son have built a robot factory. The son wants to produce lots of mechanical people to use as cheap laborers. This idea worries some people, who think the robots will be unfairly treated. These people try to shut down Rossum's factory.

Czech author and playwright Karel Capek coined the term robot *in the early twentieth century.*

However, the robots think this is a threat. They turn against their makers and on all other humans, too. After the robots cause destruction, one of them says:

Robots of the world! Many humans have fallen. We have taken the factory and we are masters of the world. The era of man has come to its end. A new epoch [age] has arisen! Domination by robots![1]

Later, the leader of the robots brags about how his race will come to dominate the world: "We will make ourselves by machine. We will erect a thousand steam machines. We will start a gush of new life from our machines. Nothing but life! Nothing but robots! Millions of robots!"[2]

Robots as Destructive Tools

Capek's idea of robots turning against humans set the scene for some of the earliest movie robots. In these films most of the robots were destructive, evil machines. One of the most famous of all movie robots came from the 1927 German film *Metropolis*. Director Fritz Lang created spectacular images of an enormous, crowded city of the future. In that city, a few wealthy individuals live in luxury, while thousands of poor people work in misery. A sinister scientist named Rotwang invents a robot with silvery metallic skin. The city's evil leader then orders him to change the creature's appearance to

One of the robots that terrified humans in the film Target Earth.

that of a beautiful woman. At the leader's orders, the disguised robot tries to encourage the workers to rebel. This gives the evil leader an excuse to attack the poor people. But luckily the workers eventually turn against the robot and destroy it.

FLASH GORDON

The theme of an evil person using robots as destructive tools was used in many later movies. Among

them were several films made in the 1930s and based on the popular comic strip "Flash Gordon." Flash is a handsome, brave space-age hero. With his girlfriend, Dale Arden, he repeatedly battles Ming the Merciless, emperor of the planet Mongo. Ming wants to conquer Earth, and he creates a race of robot soldiers called Annihilants. These robots cause death and destruction until Flash uses a remote-control device to blow them up.

Ming was not the only movie alien to use robots against humans. In the film *Target Earth* (1954), human-like robots from the planet Venus land on Earth. They have a box-like body and two arms with pincer-like fingers at the end. The robots use deadly beams of light to terrorize the people of a city. But finally a human scientist discovers a way to use sound waves to destroy them.

ROBOTS IN INDUSTRY

These early movie robots may seem unrealistic in the modern world. Most of the robots were rather simplistic **villain**s lacking personality and appeal. This was partly because few writers were taking the idea of robots seriously. The general view was that robots were just figments of the imagination.

However, in the 1940s and 1950s a few people started to take the idea of robots seriously. Among them were a handful of scientists who imagined building simple robots to use in industry. In 1954, for example, engineer George Devol invented the first industrial robot. This was a movable arm that could move items on or off a factory assembly line. Two years later, Devol and a colleague, Joseph Engleberger, started the first robot-making company, called Unimation. In the years that followed, General Motors and other large companies added robotic arms to their own assembly lines. The U.S. space agency, NASA, also created increasingly advanced robotic machines to explore the surfaces of Mars and other planets.

The famous science fiction writer Isaac Asimov (1920–1992) also took the idea of robots seriously. Like Devol, he believed that simple robots would one day become common tools in industry. Asimov also saw a future in which more-advanced robots might exist. In his view, robots would have computer-like brains and be able to copy human behavior. Years later his idea would become true— in 2000, the Honda Motor Company introduced ASIMO, a life-sized robot that can walk, climb stairs, and even serve people drinks.

ASIMOV'S LAWS

In the 1940s Asimov wrote a number of short stories about robots. These stories explore how humans and advanced robots might live together on Earth. In 1950, he collected his tales and published them under the title *I, Robot.* Now seen as a classic work, *I, Robot* contains Asimov's famous "laws of robotics." Originally, there were three laws:

Automakers and other companies now use robotic arms on their assembly lines to speed up the time it takes to produce a product.

1. A robot may not injure a human being or, through inaction, allow a human being to come to harm.
2. A robot must obey orders given it by human beings except where such orders would conflict with the First Law.
3. A robot must protect its own existence as long as such protection does not conflict with the First or Second Laws.

Later, in 1985, Asimov added a fourth robotic law: "A robot may not harm humanity or, by inaction, allow humanity to come to harm."[3]

ROBOT RELATIONSHIPS

The idea behind Asimov's robotic laws is interesting. He says that because humans make robots, they should take precautions when building them. That way, the robots cannot overpower or harm their makers.

After the publication of Asimov's laws, an increasing number of movie robots seemed to follow these rules. One of the more realistic and impressive robots was Robby in *Forbidden Planet*. Built by Dr. Morbius, caretaker of the distant planet Altair-4, Robby is designed to help humans. Robby builds houses, cooks and serves meals, and protects his human masters from harm.

Morbius programmed his mechanical servant never to harm humans. This fact is made very clear when an invisible creature tries to break into Morbius's house. Robby realizes that the creature is made by Morbius's own mind. And knowing that the intruder is a part of his master, the robot is unable to fight it. The loyal Robby remains one of the most popular of the movie robots. This is mainly because he is an example of the way in which a robot can have a good relationship with people.

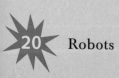

In the film The Forbidden Planet, *Robby the Robot illustrated an ideal relationship between robots and humans.*

CHAPTER 3

REALISTIC ROBOTS

E ver since the first movie robots appeared in the 1920s, filmmakers have faced a difficult challenge: How should they design these mechanical characters? Some robots, such as the one in *Metropolis*, are meant to be scary. Others, like Robby in *Forbidden Planet*, are supposed to appeal to the audience. And some robots, like C-3PO in the *Star Wars* series, are meant to be funny.

One reason why these movie robots worked so well is that the filmmakers designed them to be very believable. Audiences felt that the robots looked realistic and moved and communicated in believable ways.

Over the years filmmakers have used a variety of techniques to bring robots, like the one shown here from the Terminator *movies, to life.*

Coming to Life

A wide range of techniques have been used to make robots come to life on screen. Sometimes actors wear little or no makeup but move and speak in "robotic" ways. In *Metropolis*, for example, actress Brigitte Helm played the young woman who was really a robot in disguise. The actress wanted to show that a mechanical being was hidden beneath her character's normal-looking appearance. She used clipped, jerky movements to express this. Data, the android from *Star Trek: The Next Generation*, is another example. Data looked like a human although he had very pale skin and odd-looking eyes. But Data really came to life through his lively personality, shaped by Brent Spiner's acting skills.

Robots have also been brought to life by putting people in robot suits. Sometimes complicated mechanical and electrical devices and animation have made the robots come to life. In recent years a number of films have used computer-generated special effects to make the robots even more realistic.

Low-budget Films

The special effects needed to create a movie robot can be very expensive. In fact, robots tend to be less realistic if they appear in low-budget films. Most of the robots in low-budget films have been actors in inexpensive robot suits. These suits were usually made from the cheapest and most available

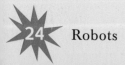

materials, such as metal pipes, scraps of wood, or even cardboard. These robots do not look very real. The Venusian robot in *Target Earth* is one example. It looks to be pieced together from cardboard boxes and exhaust hoses from a clothes dryer.

EXPENSIVE MOVIES

In contrast, films with bigger budgets can afford to make more imaginative and realistic robot suits. The mechanical woman in *Metropolis* is one of the most striking robot suits. It was created by the famous costume designer Walter Schultze-Mittendorf who first made a plaster cast of the actress's body. Then he used plastic wood to mold the robot's machine-like body. When the plastic wood dried, he removed the suit from the plaster and sprayed it with silver paint.

The finished product was so effective that it inspired a number of later filmmakers. The design for C-3PO, for example, was largely based on that of Schultze-Mittendorf's robot. Actor Anthony Daniels wore the C-3PO suit in all six *Star Wars* films and also provided the robot's voice.

Robby the Robot was also a man in a suit—this time actor Frankie Darrow. However Robby's voice was provided by Marvin Miller. The suit cost $125,000 to make in the mid-1950s. That is the same as about a million dollars today, making Robby one of the most expensive movie **props** in history. Darrow made Robby walk, but the suit

was also partly mechanical. It featured hundreds of moving parts and lights connected by some 2,600 feet (7,900m) of electrical wiring.

The Robby suit was so realistic that other film-makers later rented it for their own productions. The robots in *The Invisible Boy* (1957) and episodes of *The Twilight Zone* and a number of other television shows were all Robby (but with different names). Robby also appeared on *Lost in Space* in the 1960s. Here, Robby played opposite the show's resident robot, the B9, who was usually simply called "Robot." Here, the two robots looked very similar. This is because they were designed by the same person—the talented Robert Kinoshita.

MECHANICAL ROBOTS

R2-D2 from *Star Wars* was another mechanical movie robot. In some scenes, this famous robot had a person inside—Kenny Baker, who stands three feet eight inches (1.1m) tall. In other scenes, however, R2-D2 was a motorized metal canister. The robot moved by remote control in the same way as a remote-controlled toy racing car. There were also a number of scenes in which R2-D2 flew through the air. In these scenes the empty canister was suspended from thin but strong wires that were not visible to the audience.

Opposite: The costume that actress Brigitte Helm wore in the film Metropolis *inspired many later, cinematic robot designs.*

 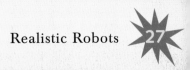

The Star Wars *robot R2-D2 was not only mechanical, but was operated by a person in some scenes.*

ANIMATION

Another technique used in some robot movies is called **stop-motion animation**. It is similar to traditional, drawn animation, in which a camera photographs a series of still drawings one at a time. These images then run through a projector at the rate of twenty-four per second. This makes it look

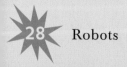

like the drawings are moving. Cartoon robots are animated in this way—one of the best known is the comical, human-hating robot Bender on the TV sitcom *Futurama* (1999–2003).

Stop-motion animation works the same way except that it uses three-dimensional models instead of drawings. In the 1987 film *RoboCop*, for example, the destructive robot ED-209 sprang to life by using stop-motion animation. Technicians built a model of the robot. They gave it arms, legs, and other body parts with many movable joints. Animator Phil Tippett positioned the model on a miniature set and photographed one **frame** of film. Then he moved the arms and legs slightly and took another image. Tippett repeated the process thousands of times. In this way, he made it look like the model robot was walking and attacking people (although it never actually moved itself).

Computer-Generated Imagery

Luckily for Tippett, there was only a single robot to animate. If the script had called for an army of ED-209s, the animation would have been far too time-consuming and expensive. This was the dilemma that the makers of *Attack of the Clones* and *I, Robot* (2004) faced. Each of these films had scenes involving hundreds and sometimes thousands of robots.

The solution was to use a computer to design, build, and animate the robots. In Computer-Generated Imagery (**CGI**), the animator draws a robot on the

computer screen. Modern computer software makes these drawings very realistic. The animator then programs the robot image to move in the desired manner. A few keystrokes can also tell the computer to copy the image, creating two, ten, fifty, or thousands of moving robots. Finally, the computer combines these images with film footage of real people, cars, or buildings. This is how the amazingly complex battle between humans and robots in the climax of *I, Robot* was created.

The use of CGI has now made it possible to

Computer-Generated Imagery was used to create the hundreds of robots seen in the film I, Robot.

create robots more realistic than the makers of *Metropolis* ever dreamed possible. But it is a tribute to them that their robot, created with far simpler tools, continues to fascinate and entertain new generations of film goers.

Chapter 4

Robots in Popular Culture

Movies about robots continue to fascinate and entertain people. One recent example is the animated film *Robots* (2005). It stars the voices of the famous actors Ewan McGregor, Halle Berry, and Mel Brooks. The action-comedy follows the adventures of a young robot named Rodney Copperbottom (with the voice of McGregor). Copperbottom wants his fellow robots to work together against evil and to make the world a better place.

The animated film Robots *is one of the most successful films made about robots.*

LIFE AFTER MOVIES

Robots was very well received by both film critics and the public and has become a **pop culture** classic. But this is only one of the many examples of popular robots in today's culture. Many of the most popular robots have come from movies. They have gone on to inspire robots in television shows such as *Lost in Space*, *Star Trek*, and the cartoon comedy series *The Jetsons* (which features a robotic maid called Rosie). The popularity of robots on screen meant that robots would soon be featured in other areas of modern culture. Thousands of robot toys appeared in the twentieth century, for instance. And hundreds more continue to be released each year. There are also kits to make both model and full-sized robots. In addition, many robotic comic book characters—some good, others evil—have been created. Famous movie robots have also inspired video games, lunchboxes, coloring books, Halloween costumes, and a host of other products.

THE HUGE TOY MARKET

The first toy robots were Robot Lilliput and Atomic Man. These were both made of tin and manufactured in Japan in the late 1940s. Robot Lilliput was

The plastic Robert the Robot was an early robot toy that was especially popular in the United States.

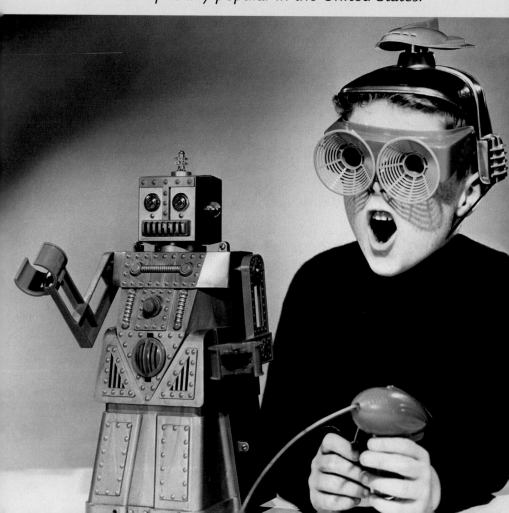

6.5 inches (16.3cm) tall and painted yellow and orange. Atomic Man, standing 5 inches (12.7cm) high, was tan and red. With their square heads and torsos, these toys looked like many of the robots in the low-budget movies of the 1930s and 1940s.

An even more popular early toy robot, Robert the Robot (not to be confused with Robby), was very popular in the United States. Robert had a square head and torso and was painted shiny silver. In 1954, Robert was the first plastic toy robot ever sold. He was manufactured by the Ideal Toy Corporation.

ADVERTISING

In the 1950s most American homes had a television. Television commercials gave toy makers a powerful new way to sell their products. Millions of American boys were thrilled by advertisements in which Robert said, "I am Robert the Robot the mechanical man. Drive me, steer me wherever you can." The toy robot had a little voice box that said these words. Children could also make him move by using a remote-control device connected to his back by a wire. Robert soon became a very popular birthday and Christmas gift.

ROBOT TOYS THROUGH THE AGES

The creation of Robby the Robot (in the mid-1950s) and the B9 (in the 1960s) inspired a new generation of toy robots. Toy manufacturers introduced smaller versions of Robby, the B9, and similar space-age robots. Plastic model kits also allowed people to make their own Robby or B9. These model kits were extremely popular with children. In the years that followed, a number of other movie robots appeared on toy store shelves. Among the more familiar were C-3PO and R2-D2 from *Star Wars*, the good and bad robots from *RoboCop*, and Rosie the maid from *The Jetsons*.

The huge robot toy market also featured products for adults. In the 1980s and 1990s, full-sized exact replicas of famous movie robots appeared. By far the most popular was the B9. One company, B9 Creations, now offers a reproduction of the B9 for $24,500. This robot moves by remote control and is also programmed to say about five hundred different phrases. Other full-sized B9s are produced every year by the B9 Builders Club. This club has more than four hundred members worldwide, several of whom have their own Web sites.

THE TRANSFORMERS

Perhaps the most popular toy robots of all are the Transformers. These robots first appeared on the market in 1984. They were made by a Japanese company called Takara. Soon afterward, Takara made a deal with the American toy company Hasbro to sell the robots in other countries. The Transformers were very popular with children and both companies enjoyed huge success.

Robots

The Transformers are advertised with the slogan "Robots in disguise!" This describes a unique feature of the robots. A child can rearrange the many plastic parts of the Transformer to make an everyday object or machine. Some Transformers can become animals. Others can be made into cars, airplanes, and ships, for example.

The Transformers are toy robots that first became popular in the 1980s. In 2007 a Transformers movie was released.

One reason the Transformers were so popular was the way they were introduced to the public. Usually, a robot appears in a movie or television show, becomes popular, and is then made into a toy. But the Transformers did the opposite. These robots started out as toys. Then a popular television show was made about them. The first Transformers series ran on television from 1984 to 1992. Its colorful characters, based on the original toy robots, took part in various adventures. Other successful television versions included *Transformers: Generation 2* (1992–1995) and *Transformers: Universe* (2003–2006). Finally, a big-budget Transformers movie, directed by Michael Bay, opened in 2007.

ROBOTIC CULTURE

The most popular robots are now featured in more than just television, movies, and toys. Many robots have become characters in comic books. Two of the largest American comic-book publishers, Marvel and DC, also invented their own robotic heroes and villains. Among Marvel's more popular robot characters are Machine Man (also called K-51), Ultron, Zero (or ADAM), and the Sentinels. DC introduced Red Tornado, Brainiac (an enemy of Superman), and Amazo, among other robots.

Another popular comic book character is Magnus, the Robot Fighter, created by Gold Key Comics. Magnus is a human who lives in A.D. 4000. His society has become dependent on robot

Robots have been popular comic book characters since the late 1930s.

workers. However, some of the robots become intelligent and want to destroy humanity, a plan Magnus tries to stop.

Robots also appear in video games. The company Activision introduced *Transformers: The Game* in 2007 at the same time as the release of the Transformers movie. There is also a video game based on the 2005 animated film *Robots*. And in 2003 Atari produced *Robot Arena: Design and Destroy*. This game allows users to create their own robots and make them fight one another in robot wars.

Today, robots are featured in thousands of movies, television shows, toys, comic books, video games, and more. This shows that people are still fascinated by robots. But it also shows how an idea that started in someone's imagination can soon become a major influence on world culture.

NOTES

CHAPTER 2: WHERE DID ROBOTS COME FROM?

1. Karel Capek, *R.U.R.: Rossum's Universal Robots*, Act 2, trans. David Wyllie. http://etext.library.adelaide.edu.au/c/capek/karel/rur/act2.html

2. Karel Capek, *R.U.R.: Rossum's Universal Robots*, Act 3, trans. David Wyllie. http://etext.library.adelaide.edu.au/c/capek/karel/rur/act3.html

3. Quoted in "The Isaac Asimov Page." http://androidworld.com/prod22.htm

Glossary

android (AN-droyed): A robot that looks very human-like.

CGI: Computer-Generated Imagery; the use of computers to create special effects for movies and television shows.

frame: One of thousands of single, still images that make up a roll of movie film.

popular (or pop) culture: The sum total of society's consumer practices (buying products), mass media (newspapers, magazines, radio, and TV), entertainment (movies, music, sports), and literature.

props: Objects used in plays or films to make a scene look realistic.

robot: A mechanical or otherwise artificial animal, person, or being.

robotic: Having to do with robots.

stop-motion animation: A film animation process in which a tiny object, animal, or person is photographed and then moved one frame at a time.

villain: A bad or evil person or character.

FOR FURTHER EXPLORATION

BOOKS

Isaac Asimov, *Robot Visions.* New York: Penguin, 2004. A collection of some of Asimov's most famous and interesting short stories about robots.

Roger Bridgman, *Robot.* London, Dorling Kindersley, 2004. An excellent introduction to robots, especially mechanical devices designed to do various forms of work.

Jeanne Cavelos, *The Science of Star Wars.* New York: St. Martin's, 2000. This fascinating book examines the scientific inventions shown in the famous *Star Wars* movies, including many kinds of robots, and discusses the real scientific principles behind each one.

Clive Gifford, *Robots.* Boston: Kingfisher, 2003. The author describes a wide range of robots, including those in movies and television programs, as well as robots used in human industry.

David Jones, *Mighty Robots: Mechanical Marvels That Fascinate and Frighten.* Toronto: Annick Press, 2005. An informative and entertaining exploration of robots, including the origin of the term robot, robots in the movies, robots in industry, and the possible use of robots in the future.

Web Sites

Isaac Asimov, "I, Robot."

http://iit.edu/~cs485/reports/asimovsi.htm

An informative site about the legendary science fiction writer and his classic book, *I, Robot.*

Todd Hertz, "Top Ten Movie Robots of All Time."

http://www.christianitytoday.com/movies/commentaries/top10movierobotsofalltime.htm

An entertaining site containing important information about each of the famous movie robots chosen by the author.

"Jeff's All Things Robot."

http://www.jeffbots.com/realbots.html#download

This comprehensive site provides a number of links to a wide range of robot-related topics, including movie and television robots, robot toys and games, robotics and robot construction, robots used in space flight, and much more.

Moviediva, "The Day the Earth Stood Still."

http://www.moviediva.com/MD_root/reviewpages/MDDayEarthStoodStill.htm

An entire site devoted to the one of the great science fiction films, with information and photos of the movie's famous and frightening robot-policeman, Gort.

INDEX

Picture Credits

Cover photo: Courtesy of photos. com

20TH CENTURY FOX / THE KOBAL COLLECTION / DIGITAL
  DOMAIN, 30-31
20TH CENTURY FOX / THE KOBAL COLLECTION, 33
AARU PRODS / THE KOBAL COLLECTION, 9
ABTCON PICTURES / THE KOBAL COLLECTION, 16
Albert L. Ortega/WireImage.com, 37
© Bettmann/CORBIS, 34
CAROLCO / THE KOBAL COLLECTION, 23
Erich Auerbach/Hulton Archive/Getty Images, 11, 14
George Rose/Getty Images Entertainment/Getty Images, 7
James Schnepf/Photographer's Choice/Getty Images, 19
LUCASFILM/20TH CENTURY FOX / THE KOBAL COLLECTION /
  HAMSHERE, KEITH, 6
LUCASFILM/20TH CENTURY FOX / THE KOBAL COLLECTION, 28
©Mary Evans Picture Library / The Image Works, 39
MGM / THE KOBAL COLLECTION, 21
UFA / THE KOBAL COLLECTION, 26

ABOUT THE AUTHOR

In addition to his acclaimed volumes on ancient civilizations, historian and award-winning writer Don Nardo has written or edited many books about strange phenomena, including famous monsters. These include volumes on the mythical snake-headed Medusa, the legendary one-eyed Cyclops, invading Martians of literature and movies, the possible existence of extraterrestrial life, and numerous books about the non-human creatures of ancient Egyptian, Greek, Roman, Persian, and Nordic mythology. Mr. Nardo lives with his wife Christine in Massachusetts.